60 RECIPES **1 SHEET OF PUFF PASTRY** **1 BAKING TRAY**

PUFF IT UP

CAITLIN MACDONALD

photography by Luke Albert

Quadrille

CONTENTS

9 Introduction

12

TOP IT

46

TWIST IT

70

ROLL IT

90

FILL IT

114

DECORATE IT

136 Index
140 Acknowledgements
141 Author bio

Introduction

This book is a celebration of puff pastry – specifically the shop-bought, ready-to-roll kind. While I love making puff pastry from scratch – and would encourage you to try this too (it's easier than you think!) – you can't argue with the great results you get from the ready-rolled stuff you can buy from the chillers in supermarkets.

The following chapters are full of recipes that will show you, or even just remind you, of the myriad different things you can cook with this versatile ingredient – from sweet tarts to savoury twists, sausage rolls to pies, you can make snacks and canapés, use it for everyday eating or glam it up for special occasions.

Simple steps for perfect puffs

These recipes are written to be straightforward, affordable (apart from a couple of slightly more indulgent ones) and, best of all, quick. Almost every recipe uses just one sheet of puff pastry and one baking tray (with a couple of exceptions that can be cooked in batches), and all can be easily made by hand – one or two call for a food processor, if you have one.

Although each recipe instructs you to line the baking tray with baking parchment, packets of pastry come with their own parchment, so you can just unroll the pastry and paper and place it straight onto the baking sheet, if you like. This is a great solution if you are topping the whole pastry sheet and baking it, but you might prefer to line the tray with fresh parchment for recipes that require cutting the pastry into parcels or shapes.

Each recipe uses 10 ingredients or fewer, and needs no cooking other than turning on the oven, so you'll have a delicious meal or snack ready in less than an hour, with very little washing up to do afterwards.

Keeping your pastry as cold as possible is important, so try to work fairly swiftly with it and remember you can always return it to the fridge to cool down again before baking if it starts to feel too warm.

Making the recipes your own

These recipes can be adapted to suit whatever ingredients are in season, what you might have in your cupboards and the back of your fridge that need using up, or just your favourite ingredients and flavours.

However, while puff pastry is fairly forgiving, if you are adjusting any of the recipes to use alternative ingredients, be wary of how wet ingredients interact with the pastry – we want crisp, flaky pastry, not soggy, uncooked-tasting pastry. Most of the recipes that have toppings require the pastry to be pre-baked in order to prevent this, so use your instincts; if in doubt, cook for a few minutes longer. I'd always rather have extra crunch, so keep an eye on your bake and use foil to cover the toppings to prevent them overcooking, if necessary.

The recipes are customisable to suit different ages, diets and preferences – if you are making a plant-based dish, all shop-bought puff pastry should be plant-based, unless labelled all-butter, so check the packaging to be certain. You could also use gluten-free puff pastry, if you'd like.

It's also important to remember that ovens can really vary, so cook these recipes according to the timings and temperatures recommended, but keep an eye on your bakes and don't be afraid to cook them a little longer or shorter than suggested depending on your oven. You could also use an oven thermometer for ultimate temperature accuracy, if you have one.

When choosing your ingredients, go for the best quality you can – for example, choose free-range eggs and flaky sea salt to finish your bakes.

Use this book for all cravings and any occasion: speedy weeknight dinners, prep-ahead snacks for lunchboxes or picnics, canapés for a party, fun weekend breakfasts and easy puddings – there is something for everyone.

Happy cooking!

TOP

IT

Mushroom and egg tart

SERVES 4–6

This tart is great to throw together if you want something different on your breakfast table. It's quick to assemble and is very hands-off compared to a classic full breakfast. Plus, you can really adjust the toppings to suit whatever you can find at the back of your fridge – switch the bacon out for sausages or chorizo, get rid of the mushrooms if you're not a fan, or throw some cheese on there if you fancy it.

100g (3½oz) cherry tomatoes, cut in half
1 x 320g (11¼oz) sheet of puff pastry
5 eggs
50g (2oz) crème fraîche
2 tablespoons wholegrain mustard
2 portobello mushrooms, sliced
4 rashers streaky bacon, cut into 2 shorter pieces
10g (¼oz) fresh tarragon, leaves picked
Salt and freshly ground black pepper, to taste

Preheat the oven to 200°C/180°C fan/400°F and line a baking tray with baking parchment. Sprinkle the tomato halves with a little salt and lay, cut-side down, on some kitchen paper to drain some of their liquid.

Take the puff pastry out of the fridge and score a 2cm (¾in) border right round the sheet, being careful not to cut through the pastry. Beat one of the eggs in a bowl and brush the pastry sheet all over with it. Transfer to the oven to bake for an initial 10 minutes.

Meanwhile, mix the crème fraîche and mustard together, seasoning generously with salt and pepper. Remove the pastry from the oven and gently press down the middle where it has puffed up. Spread the crème fraîche mixture over the middle up to the scored border, then arrange the sliced mushrooms, cherry tomatoes and bacon over the top, leaving four gaps for the remaining eggs to be cracked into later. Transfer to the oven for another 15 minutes.

After this time, remove from the oven and carefully crack the remaining eggs into the gaps. Return to the oven for a final 10–12 minutes, or until the eggs are cooked and the pastry is golden.

Scatter the tarragon over the top and crack over plenty of black pepper. Cut into slices and serve.

Triple cheese and spinach pie

SERVES 4–6

This tart is really one for the cheese lovers. It's sort of quiche-like but the spinach, cheese and Aleppo chilli are a nod to Turkish pide flavours I've had before. Serve with a fresh, lemony salad to balance out the richness.

200g (7oz) baby spinach

1 x 320g (11¼oz) sheet of puff pastry

3 eggs

200g (7oz) crème fraîche

80g (3oz) Cheddar, grated

80g (3oz) mozzarella, grated

80g (3oz) feta, crumbled

2 spring onions (scallions), thinly sliced

1 garlic clove, minced

2 teaspoons Aleppo chilli flakes

Salt and freshly ground black pepper, to taste

Preheat the oven to 200°C/180°C fan/400°F and line a baking tray with baking parchment.

Put the spinach into a colander and place in the sink. Boil the kettle, then pour the boiling water over the spinach to wilt. Run under cold water to cool, then drain and squeeze out as much liquid as you can and roughly chop.

Unroll the puff pastry onto the lined baking tray and use a sharp knife to cut two strips off the shorter ends of the sheet, each about 2.5cm (1in) thick, then lay these on top of the same ends. Fold the long edges of the pastry over to make a crust lengthways too, then press it down well to seal. Beat one of the eggs in a bowl, then brush it all over the pastry. Transfer to the oven to bake for 10 minutes, then use a spoon to gently press the centre down where it will have puffed up.

Meanwhile, mix the remaining two eggs, crème fraîche, cheeses, chopped spinach, spring onions, garlic and chilli flakes until well combined, then season with a little salt and pepper. Spoon this mixture into the middle of the pre-baked pastry, making sure it doesn't spill out onto the crust. Return to the oven for 20–25 minutes until golden on top and the mixture has set.

Leave to stand for 10 minutes before cutting into slices to serve.

Hot smoked trout and cream cheese tart

SERVES 4–6

¼ red onion, thinly sliced
Zest and juice of 1 lemon
1 x 320g (11¼oz) sheet of puff
  pastry
1 egg, beaten
200g (7oz) cream cheese
150g (5oz) thick Greek
  yoghurt
¼ cucumber, thinly sliced
100g (3½oz) hot smoked trout
  or salmon, flaked
2 tablespoons capers
Handful of rocket (arugula)
Salt and freshly ground black
  pepper, to taste

Baking a sheet of puff pastry and then topping it with cold ingredients makes for the perfect, easy, fresh lunch. This tart is inspired by a lox bagel, but you can use the cream cheese as a starting point and top with whatever is in season. I love marinated tomatoes with black olives and lots of herbs.

Preheat the oven to 200°C/180°C fan/400°F and line a baking tray with baking parchment.

Add the red onion to a small bowl and squeeze over the juice of ½ lemon. Add a pinch of salt then scrunch together with your hands. Set aside to pickle.

Unroll the puff pastry onto the lined baking tray and score a 2cm (¾in) border right round the sheet, being careful not to cut right through the pastry. Brush the beaten egg all over the pastry. Transfer to the oven to bake for about 20 minutes, or until the pastry is golden brown and puffed up.

In the meantime, whisk the cream cheese with the Greek yoghurt and zest of ½ lemon. Season to taste with salt and plenty of black pepper.

Remove the pastry from the oven and use a spoon to gently press the centre down where it will have puffed up. Leave to cool.

Spread the whipped cream cheese over the middle of the pastry, then top with the cucumber slices. Arrange the smoked trout all over, then scatter the capers and pickled red onion all around. Finish with the rocket leaves and lots of freshly ground black pepper, then cut into slices. Cut the remaining leftover lemon half into wedges and serve alongside the tart to squeeze over.

Cheese and tomato tartlets

MAKES 6

These little galettes are delicious straight out of the oven, but are just as good for packed lunches. I like Marmite in mine, but feel free to use mustard, pesto or a chutney, if you prefer!

2 large tomatoes (beef or heirloom, for example)
1 x 320g (11¼oz) sheet of puff pastry
3 teaspoons Marmite or 3 tablespoons mustard
120g (4oz) Cheddar, finely grated
3 teaspoons dried thyme
1 egg, beaten
Salt and freshly ground black pepper, to taste

Preheat the oven to 200°C/180°C fan/400°F and line a baking tray with baking parchment.

Cut the tomatoes into thick slices (three from each tomato) and sprinkle with some salt, then lay on kitchen paper to drain some of their liquid.

Unroll the puff pastry and cut into six pieces. Do this by halving the sheet into two long strips then cutting each of those into three. For each piece of pastry, spread your chosen condiment over the centre, then add a pile of cheese – reserving a little for the crusts. Lay the tomato slices on top and sprinkle over the thyme along with some salt and pepper. Gently fold the edges up to encase the tomato slices, overlapping the pastry as needed – don't worry about it being neat or if the pastry breaks a little. Lift them on to the lined baking tray and brush with the beaten egg, then sprinkle the reserved cheese over the crusts. Slide into the oven and bake for 25–35 minutes until golden.

Courgette and goat's cheese tart

SERVES 4–6

I love making this tart in the summer and serving it alongside a big salad. It tastes even better once cooled, so this is a great dish to make ahead or pack for a picnic.

1 x 320g (11¼oz) sheet of puff pastry
1 egg, beaten
125g (4½oz) ricotta
125g (4½oz) soft goat's cheese
Zest and juice of ½ lemon
200g (7oz) courgette (zucchini), thinly sliced
2 garlic cloves, minced
½ teaspoon chilli flakes
2 tablespoons extra virgin olive oil
30g (1oz) pistachios, roughly chopped
Honey, to drizzle
Salt and freshly ground black pepper, to taste

Preheat the oven to 200°C/180°C fan/400°F and line a baking tray with baking parchment.

Unroll the puff pastry sheet onto the lined baking tray and use a sharp knife to score a 2cm (¾in) border right round the sheet, being careful not to cut right through. Brush all over with the beaten egg, then transfer to the oven to bake for an initial 10 minutes.

Mix the ricotta and goat's cheese together until smooth, then season to taste with the lemon juice, salt and pepper. Toss the courgette with the lemon zest, garlic, chilli flakes, olive oil and a pinch of salt.

Remove the pastry from the oven and use a spoon to gently press down the middle where it has puffed up. Spread the goat's cheese mix over the centre, then arrange the courgette slices over the top. Spoon any leftover oil from the courgettes over the top, then put back in the oven for 20–30 minutes until golden.

Scatter over the chopped pistachios and drizzle with honey, then serve.

Pepperoni pizza tart

SERVES 4–6

This recipe really hits the spot when you want homemade pizza but don't have the time to make dough. The puff pastry works so well as a base, and you can top it with your favourite ingredients. This quick tomato sauce is great, but try using crème fraîche mixed with Parmesan for a white base, too.

400g (14oz) tin good-quality plum tomatoes, liquid drained

3 tablespoons extra virgin olive oil

½ tablespoon dried oregano

1 x 320g (11¼oz) sheet of puff pastry

1 egg, beaten

70g (2¾oz) pepperoni or salami

125g (4½oz) mozzarella, drained and sliced

Handful of fresh basil leaves

10g (¼oz) Parmesan, finely grated (optional)

Salt and freshly ground black pepper, to taste

Preheat the oven to 200°C/180°C fan/400°F and line a baking tray with baking parchment.

Tip the plum tomatoes into a large mixing bowl and use your hands to crush them. Add 2 tablespoons of the olive oil, the oregano and a generous pinch of salt and pepper. Taste to check the seasoning, adjusting as needed.

Unroll the puff pastry onto the lined baking tray and use a small knife to score an approximately 2cm (¾in) border right round the sheet, being careful not to cut all the way through the pastry. Brush the entire sheet with the beaten egg, then transfer to the oven to cook for an initial 10 minutes.

Remove the pastry from the oven and use a spoon to gently press down the centre where it will have puffed up. Spoon the tomato sauce over the centre, then arrange the pepperoni and mozzarella on top. Drizzle the remaining tablespoon of olive oil over the top, then return to the oven for a further 10–15 minutes until golden and the cheese is bubbling.

Scatter over the basil leaves and Parmesan, if using, then cut into slices to serve.

Anchovy, onion and tomato tart

SERVES 4–6

This tart has all the classic flavours of a Pissaladière Niçoise, but with the addition of tomatoes. Replace the anchovies with capers, if you prefer.

200g (7oz) medium tomatoes on the vine, thinly sliced
1 x 320g (11¼oz) sheet of puff pastry
1 egg, beaten
½ onion, very thinly sliced
80g (3oz) anchovy fillets, drained
50g (2oz) pitted black olives
2 tablespoons extra virgin olive oil
Salt and freshly ground black pepper, to taste
10g (¼oz) fresh chives, finely chopped, to serve

Preheat the oven to 200°C/180°C fan/400°F and line a baking tray with baking parchment.

Lay the tomato slices on some kitchen paper and sprinkle generously with salt. Leave for 10–15 minutes to drain some of their liquid.

Unroll the puff pastry onto the lined baking tray and use a small knife to score an approximately 2cm (¾in) border right round the sheet, being careful not to cut all the way through. Brush all over with the beaten egg, then lay the onion and tomato slices over the top. Arrange the anchovies in a criss-cross pattern, placing the olives evenly in the gaps. Drizzle over the olive oil and transfer to the oven to cook for 20–25 minutes until golden brown.

Sprinkle the chives over the top of the cooked tart to serve.

Tartiflette pie

SERVES 4–6

One of my favourite things in the world to eat is tartiflette. It's a cheesy, potato dish from the Haute-Savoie region in France and is so comforting on a cold day. This tart is very untraditional but incredibly delicious. Serve with a mustard- and lemon-heavy salad to balance out the richness, and, of course, extra cornichons.

1 x 320g (11¼oz) sheet of puff pastry
1 egg, beaten
150g (5oz) crème fraîche
½ onion, very thinly sliced
50ml (2fl oz) white wine
100g (3½oz) Charlotte potatoes, cut into 2mm (⅛in) slices
150g (5oz) lardons or diced pancetta
100g (3½oz) Reblochon (Camembert or Brie would be good substitutions), cut into slices
50g (2oz) cornichons, halved lengthways
Salt and freshly ground black pepper, to taste

Preheat the oven to 200°C/180°C fan/400°F and line a baking tray with baking parchment.

Unroll the puff pastry onto the lined baking tray and use a small knife to score an approximately 2cm (¾in) border right round the sheet, being careful not to cut all the way through. Brush all over with the beaten egg, then transfer to the oven to bake for 10 minutes.

Mix the crème fraîche, onion and white wine until well combined, then season with some salt and pepper.

Remove the pastry from the oven and use a spoon to gently press down the centre where it has puffed up. Spread the crème fraîche mix over the centre and arrange the potato slices on top. Scatter the lardons all over, then lay over the slices of cheese. Transfer to the oven and bake for 25–30 minutes until the cheese is bubbling and the pastry is golden.

To finish, top with the cornichons then cut into slices to serve.

See images on pages 28–29.

Pumpkin, blue cheese and hazelnut tart

SERVES 4–6

This tart is best made in autumn when you can get your hands on some really delicious pumpkin. If you aren't a fan of blue cheese but still want something punchy, use taleggio instead.

220g (8oz) pumpkin or butternut squash, very thinly sliced on a mandoline
2 tablespoons extra virgin olive oil
2 garlic cloves, minced
1 x 320g (11¼oz) sheet of puff pastry
100g (3½oz) crème fraîche
150g (5oz) St Agur or other blue cheese
15 fresh sage leaves, larger ones torn
30g (1oz) toasted hazelnuts, roughly chopped
Salt and freshly ground black pepper, to taste

Preheat the oven to 200°C/180°C fan/400°F and line a baking tray with baking parchment.

Toss the pumpkin slices in a bowl with the olive oil, garlic and a little salt and pepper.

Unroll the puff pastry onto the lined baking tray and use a sharp knife to score a 2cm (¾in) border right round the sheet, being careful not to cut all the way through. Spread the crème fraîche all over, including over the border pastry, then break the cheese into chunks and dot evenly inside the border. Lay the pumpkin slices over the top so they overlap slightly, then spoon over any olive oil left in the bowl. Transfer to the oven for 25 minutes.

After this time, remove from the oven and scatter over the sage leaves. Return to the oven for a further 10–15 minutes, or until the pastry is golden and the pumpkin cooked.

Scatter the hazelnuts over the top and leave the tart to sit for 10 minutes before cutting into slices.

See images on pages 32–33.

Spiced carrot and whipped tofu tart with coriander chutney

SERVES 4–6

This vegan tart packs so much flavour with just a few ingredients! Whipping the tofu takes just a minute, but it adds protein to this dish and creates a delicious base for the carrots. The chutney really takes this to the next level, so don't skip it.

350g (12oz) carrots, peeled and cut into 2cm (¾in) rounds

2 tablespoons curry paste of choice

400g (14oz) block of firm tofu, drained

5 tablespoons extra virgin olive oil

1 x 320g (11¼oz) sheet of puff pastry

30g (1oz) fresh coriander (cilantro)

10g (¼oz) fresh mint, leaves picked

Juice of ½ lemon

½ red onion, finely diced

2–3 tablespoons dairy-free yoghurt

2–3 tablespoons tamarind chutney

Salt and freshly ground black pepper, to taste

Preheat the oven to 200°C/180°C fan/400°F and line a baking tray with baking parchment.

Toss the sliced carrots with the curry paste and season with salt and pepper. Add the tofu to a food processor with 1 tablespoon of the olive oil and blitz until broken down and fairly smooth. Season to taste.

Unroll the puff pastry onto the lined baking tray and score a 2cm (¾in) border right round the sheet, being careful not to cut right through the pastry. Spread the whipped tofu over the middle then top with the carrot slices. Drizzle 2 tablespoons of the olive oil over the tart, including the border. Transfer to the oven to cook for 30–40 minutes until the carrots are cooked through.

In the meantime, add the coriander (reserving a few leaves to garnish), mint, lemon juice and remaining 2 tablespoons of olive oil to a blender along with a splash of water. Blitz until smooth, seasoning to taste with salt and pepper.

Remove the tart from the oven and scatter over the red onion and reserved coriander leaves. Drizzle the coriander chutney, yoghurt and tamarind chutney all over to serve.

Roasted tomato and tuna tart

SERVES 4–6

This recipe heroes simple ingredients but makes a really satisfying and fresh lunch. If you want to prep this ahead, wait to add the tuna, rocket and vinaigrette until just before serving.

300g (10½oz) cherry tomatoes, cut in half

1 x 320g (11¼oz) sheet of puff pastry

1 egg, beaten

100g (3½oz) crème fraîche

2 tablespoons Dijon mustard

½ red onion, thinly sliced

2 tablespoons capers

3 tablespoons extra virgin olive oil

1 tablespoon white wine vinegar

220g (8oz) jar of tuna in oil, drained

Handful of rocket (arugula) leaves

Salt and freshly ground black pepper, to taste

Preheat the oven to 200°C/180°C fan/400°F and line a baking tray with baking parchment.

Sprinkle the halved cherry tomatoes with some salt and lay cut-side down on some kitchen paper to draw out some of their liquid.

Unroll the puff pastry onto the lined baking tray and use a small knife to score a roughly 2cm (¾in) border right round the sheet. Brush all over with the beaten egg, then transfer to the oven to bake for an initial 10 minutes. Meanwhile, mix the crème fraîche with 1 tablespoon of Dijon mustard and season with a little salt and pepper.

Remove the pastry from the oven and use a spoon to gently press down the middle where it has puffed up. Spread the crème fraîche mixture over the centre, then lay the tomatoes on top, cut-side up. Add the onion and capers around the tomatoes, then drizzle with 1 tablespoon of olive oil and season with salt and pepper. Return to the oven to cook for another 20 minutes.

Mix the remaining olive oil and mustard with the vinegar until well combined, then season with salt and pepper.

Remove the tart from the oven, then break over the tuna and scatter the rocket. Drizzle with the vinaigrette to finish.

Lahmacun-inspired tart

SERVES 4–6

Inspired by lahmacun (sometimes known as Turkish pizza), this tart hits the spot when you want something hearty but also fresh. Serve with a herby chopped salad.

300g (10½oz) beef mince (ground beef) (at least 15% fat)
1 red onion, half finely chopped and half thinly sliced
2 tablespoons tomato purée (paste)
2 teaspoons allspice
2 teaspoons Aleppo chilli flakes
3 tablespoons extra virgin olive oil
1 x 320g (11¼oz) sheet of puff pastry
50g (2oz) tahini
Juice of 1 lemon
2 large vine tomatoes, cut into chunks
Small bunch of fresh parsley, roughly chopped
Salt and freshly ground black pepper, to taste

Preheat the oven to 200°C/180°C fan/400°F and line a baking tray with baking parchment.

Mix the beef, finely chopped red onion, tomato purée, allspice, chilli flakes, 1 tablespoon of olive oil and some salt together until well combined.

Take the puff pastry out of the fridge and score a 2cm (¾in) border, being careful not to cut through the pastry. Brush the scored pastry sheet with 1 tablespoon of the olive oil, then transfer to the oven to bake for an initial 10 minutes.

Use the back of a spoon to press down the pastry in the middle where it has puffed up, then press the beef mixture on top in an even layer. Return to the oven for a further 20–25 minutes until the meat is cooked and the pastry golden brown.

Meanwhile, make the tahini sauce by whisking together the tahini, remaining 1 tablespoon of olive oil, juice of ½ the lemon and 1 tablespoon of water until smooth. Season to taste with salt.

Remove the tart from the oven and top with the sliced red onion and tomatoes. Drizzle over the tahini sauce and scatter with parsley to finish. Serve with an extra squeeze of lemon, if you like.

Banoffee tart

SERVES 8

This banoffee tart delivers all the deliciousness of a banoffee pie for half the time and effort. Bake the puff pastry in advance and you've got a speedy pudding when you're hosting dinner.

1 x 320g (11¼oz) sheet of puff pastry
1 egg, beaten
4 ripe bananas
200g (7oz) caramel sauce or dulce de leche
1 tablespoon white miso
300ml (10fl oz) double (heavy) cream
1 teaspoon vanilla bean paste
3 ginger nut biscuits, crushed
Dark (semisweet) chocolate, to grate

Preheat the oven to 200°C/180°C fan/400°F and line a baking tray with baking parchment.

Unroll the puff pastry onto the lined baking tray and use a sharp knife to score a 2cm (¾in) border, being careful not to cut all the way through. Brush all over with the egg and transfer to the oven to bake for 20–25 minutes or until golden. Remove from the oven and set aside to cool.

Meanwhile, prepare the toppings. First, add two of the bananas to a bowl and use a fork to mash really well. Add the caramel and miso and mix until well combined. Slice the remaining two bananas into 1cm (½in) rounds. In a separate bowl, whip the cream and vanilla bean paste to soft peaks.

Spread the banana caramel over the middle of the pastry, then top with the sliced banana. Add spoonfuls of the whipped cream over the top, then scatter over the crushed ginger nuts. Grate over some dark chocolate to finish, then cut into slices to serve.

Peach galette with honey and yoghurt cream

SERVES 8

Make this tart in the summer months for a delicious dessert. Try using herbs instead of cardamom, if you like – basil or tarragon would be really delicious here. Just blitz a small handful of leaves with the sugar before tossing with the fruit.

4 peaches or nectarines, stone removed and cut into wedges
30g (1oz) caster (superfine) sugar
8 cardamom pods, seeds removed and ground
1 tablespoon cornflour (cornstarch)
1 x 320g (11¼oz) sheet of puff pastry
1 egg, beaten
1 tablespoon demerara sugar
100g (3½oz) double (heavy) cream
200g (7oz) very thick Greek yoghurt
2 tablespoons runny honey
Salt and freshly ground black pepper, to taste

Preheat the oven to 180°C/160°C fan/350°F and line a baking tray with baking parchment.

Start by preparing the peaches. In a mixing bowl, toss the peach wedges with the sugar, cardamom and cornflour.

Unroll the puff pastry onto the lined baking tray and, working fairly quickly, arrange the peach wedges around the pastry sheet, leaving a 5cm (2in) border right round the sheet. Once you have added the fruit, begin to fold the edges up to encase the fruit, overlapping the pastry as you fold around and not worrying about being neat – rustic-looking is good! Brush the edges with the beaten egg and sprinkle the demerara sugar all over.

Bake in the oven for 30–40 minutes until the pastry is golden brown and the fruit is juicy and soft, but still holding its shape.

While the galette cooks, in a bowl, whip together the cream, yoghurt and honey to soft peaks.

Slice the galette and serve warm, with the yoghurt cream spooned over.

Strawberry and goat's cheese tart

SERVES 6–8

Cheese and jam on toast is one of my favourite snacks. I would usually use mature Cheddar and raspberry jam, but this strawberry and goat's cheese tart feels like a more sophisticated version.

1 x 320g (11¼oz) sheet of puff pastry
1 egg, beaten
60g (2½oz) crème fraîche
Juice of ½ lemon
400g (14oz) strawberries, sliced
20g (¾oz) caster (superfine) sugar
1½ tablespoons cornflour (cornstarch)
75g (3oz) soft goat's cheese
Salt and freshly ground black pepper, to taste
Handful of fresh basil leaves, to garnish
Good-quality balsamic vinegar, to drizzle

Preheat the oven to 180°C/160°C fan/350°F and line a baking tray with baking parchment.

Unroll the puff pastry onto the lined baking tray and score a 2cm (¾in) border right round the sheet, being careful not to cut the whole way through. Brush it all over with the egg and transfer to the oven to bake for an initial 10 minutes.

In the meantime, mix the crème fraîche with the lemon juice and some black pepper. Add the strawberries to a separate bowl with the sugar and cornflour and toss gently to combine.

Remove the pastry from the oven and spread the crème fraîche over the middle. Dot the goat's cheese around the pastry, then arrange the strawberries on top. Return to the oven for 25–30 minutes until the pastry is golden and the strawberries are softened and jammy.

Scatter the basil leaves over the top and drizzle with balsamic vinegar to finish.

Apple crumble tart

SERVES 8

This tart has all the best bits of apple desserts: flaky pastry, jammy fruit and buttery, oaty crumble. Eat warm with ice cream, cold custard or cream for a perfect winter pud.

50g (2oz) plain (all purpose) flour

50g (2oz) rolled oats

50g (2oz) soft light brown sugar, plus 2 tablespoons

50g (2oz) unsalted butter, cut into cubes

Juice of ½ lemon

3 Granny Smith apples

1 teaspoon ground cinnamon

1 x 320g (11¼oz) sheet of puff pastry

1 egg, beaten

Apricot jam or honey, to glaze (optional)

Preheat the oven to 200°C/180°C fan/400°F and line a baking tray with baking parchment.

Make the crumble topping by combining the flour, oats, 50g (2oz) of sugar, butter and a good pinch of salt in a bowl. Use your fingertips to rub together until the mixture resembles breadcrumbs, leaving a few larger chunks of butter. Transfer to the fridge while you prepare the apples.

Fill a mixing bowl with cold water and squeeze in the lemon juice. Peel and core the apples, then cut into fairly thin slices. Put them straight into the lemon water to prevent them discolouring. Once they are all cut, drain and then dry the slices as much as you can, before tossing with the remaining 2 tablespoons of sugar and the cinnamon.

Unroll the puff pastry onto the lined baking tray and arrange the apple slices all over, leaving a 2cm (¾in) border right round the sheet. Fold the edges up over the fruit to contain any juices, then top with the crumble mixture. Brush the folded edges with the beaten egg, then transfer to the oven to bake for 35–40 minutes.

If using, mix a couple of tablespoons of jam or honey with a splash of boiling water to loosen. Remove the tart from the oven and brush liberally with this to make glossy, then allow to cool for 10 minutes before cutting into slices. Serve with ice cream, custard or cream

TWIST

IT

Green chilli cheese swirl

SERVES 8

One of my favourite bakeries in London, The Dusty Knuckle, does this incredible breakfast sandwich, comprising a fried egg, cheese, green chilli and coriander. This recipe was inspired by that sandwich, with the addition of onion (of course) and warming cumin seeds.

350g (12oz) tinned or leftover boiled potatoes, drained
100g (3½oz) Cheddar, grated
100g (3½oz) mozzarella, torn or grated
100g (3½oz) ricotta
1 red onion, finely chopped
2 teaspoons cumin seeds
2 green chillies, finely chopped
10g (¼oz) fresh coriander (cilantro), roughly chopped
2 eggs
1 x 320g (11¼oz) sheet of puff pastry
Salt and freshly ground black pepper, to taste

Preheat the oven to 200°C/180°C fan/400°F and line a baking tray with baking parchment.

Add the potatoes to a large mixing bowl and use a fork to crush them. Add the Cheddar, mozzarella, ricotta, red onion, 1 teaspoon cumin seeds, green chillies and coriander, then mix well until combined. Crack in one of the eggs and mix again, then season generously with salt and pepper. Lightly beat the other egg in a small bowl.

Unroll the pastry on a work surface and cut it in half to make two long strips. Place half the potato mixture along the middle of each strip in a sausage shape, then lift one side of the pastry up and over the filling. Brush the edge with the reserved beaten egg, then lift the other side up and press together to seal. Repeat with the other half.

Gently lift one of the sausages and lay it, seal-side down, on the lined baking tray. Curl the pastry into a swirl, attaching the end of the first to the second one and curling that round too. Brush the entire thing with egg, scatter with the remaining cumin seeds and transfer to the oven for 30–40 minutes until golden.

Mustard and Cheddar twists

MAKES 12

Making your own cheese twists at home is so easy. Using just a few ingredients that you likely have in the fridge already, these are the perfect pre-dinner nibble.

1 x 320g (11¼oz) sheet of puff pastry
3 tablespoons wholegrain mustard
120g (4oz) Cheddar, grated
1 egg, beaten

Preheat the oven to 200°C/180°C fan/400°F and line a baking tray with baking parchment.

Unroll the puff pastry and spread the mustard all over it. Sprinkle over the grated cheese, then fold the sheet in half as if you're closing a book. Use a rolling pin to roll the folded pastry out a little, then cut into 12 strips. Twist each strip a few times and put onto the lined baking tray.

Brush with the beaten egg and transfer to the oven to bake for 20–25 minutes until crisp and golden.

Prosciutto and asparagus twists with dippy eggs

MAKES 12

Make these for a fun weekend breakfast. They're great for dipping into soft-boiled eggs, but would be delicious served with scrambled, and really special with poached and hollandaise sauce.

12 asparagus spears (chunkier is better here)
6 slices of prosciutto, halved lengthways
1 x 320g (11¼oz) sheet of puff pastry
2 tablespoons wholegrain mustard
1 egg, beaten

Preheat the oven to 180°C/160°C fan/350°F and line a baking tray with baking parchment.

Wrap each asparagus spear with a piece of prosciutto.

Unroll the puff pastry sheet and spread the mustard over it. Cut into 12 strips, then twist a piece of pastry around each asparagus spear before placing them on the lined baking tray.

Brush them with the egg and bake in the oven for 15–20 minutes until the pastry is puffed up and golden.

See images on pages 52–53.

Cheese and chutney twists

MAKES 12

A cheese and chutney sandwich is so simple but incredibly satisfying. Those flavours are used here and are just as good in puff pastry form.

1 x 320g (11¼oz) sheet of puff pastry
3 tablespoons chutney of choice
120g (4oz) Cheddar, grated
1 egg, beaten
2 teaspoons nigella seeds

Preheat the oven to 200°C/180°C fan/400°F and line a baking tray with baking parchment.

Unroll the puff pastry and spread the chutney all over. Sprinkle over the grated cheese, then fold the sheet in half as if you're closing a book. Use a rolling pin to roll the folded pastry out a little, then cut into 12 strips. Twist each strip a few times and put onto the lined baking tray.

Brush with the beaten egg, scatter over the nigella seeds and bake in the oven for 20–25 minutes until crisp and golden.

'Nduja and Parmesan twists

MAKES 12

A spicy spin on a classic cheese twist. Best enjoyed with a cold beer in the sun!

1 x 320g (11¼oz) sheet of puff pastry
75g (3oz) 'nduja (or less if you'd prefer them not too spicy)
30g (1½oz) Parmesan, finely grated
Zest of ½ lemon
1 egg, beaten

Preheat the oven to 200°C/180°C fan/400°F and line a baking tray with baking parchment.

Unroll the puff pastry and spread the 'nduja all over. Sprinkle over the Parmesan and zest the lemon, then fold the sheet in half as if you're closing a book. Cut into 12 strips, then twist each one a few times and put onto a lined baking tray.

Brush with the beaten egg and transfer to the oven to cook for 20–25 minutes until crisp and golden.

Broccoli and anchovy twists

MAKES 12

These are full of flavour and goodness from the broccoli. Serve with a garlicky yoghurt or lemon mayo for dipping.

12 Tenderstem broccoli spears
2 tablespoons extra virgin olive oil
1 x 320g (11¼oz) sheet of puff pastry
1 x 50g (2oz) tin of anchovies, drained
30g (1oz) Parmesan, finely grated
1 egg, beaten

Preheat the oven to 200°C/180°C fan/400°F and line a baking tray with baking parchment. Toss the broccoli with the olive oil, ensuring every piece is well coated.

Unroll the puff pastry and arrange the anchovies over one half. Sprinkle over the Parmesan, then lift the other half of the pastry over to cover, as if you're closing a book. Lightly press down to seal, then cut into 12 strips.

Wrap a pastry strip around each piece of broccoli then lay them down on the baking tray. Brush them with the beaten egg, then bake in the oven for 20 minutes until the pastry is golden and puffed up.

Halloumi and mango chutney parcels

MAKES 16

These sweet and salty halloumi dippers are so moreish and will go down a treat at any party. Be generous with the mango chutney and serve with extra for dipping, too.

2 x 225g (8oz) blocks of halloumi
1 x 320g (11¼oz) sheet of puff pastry
4 tablespoons mango chutney
1 egg, beaten
1 tablespoon nigella or cumin seeds

Preheat the oven to 200°C/180°C fan/400°F. Line a baking tray with baking parchment.

Cut each halloumi block into eight sticks. Unroll the puff pastry and cut it into four long strips, then cut each strip into four squares. Add a little mango chutney to each square, then turn them so you are looking at a diamond shape. Add a halloumi stick to the centre of each one, then twist the pastry round to seal.

Place on the baking tray and brush with the beaten egg, then sprinkle over the nigella or cumin seeds. Bake in the oven for 20–25 minutes until golden. Serve immediately while the halloumi is hot.

Honey mustard pigs in blankets

MAKES 24

I've diverged from the classic bacon-wrapped pigs in blankets we are used to having in the UK and opted for the pastry-wrapped version found in the US. With the addition of sweet and sticky honey mustard, these just might tempt you to change things up at your next festive meal.

½ tablespoon Dijon mustard
1 tablespoon wholegrain mustard
1 tablespoon honey
1 sprig of fresh rosemary, leaves stripped and finely chopped
12 chipolatas
1 x 320g (11¼oz) sheet of puff pastry
1 egg, beaten

Preheat the oven to 200°C/180°C fan/400°F and line a baking tray with baking parchment.

Mix the Dijon and wholegrain mustard with the honey, then stir in the rosemary. Twist each chipolata in the middle so it divides into two, then cut in half so you have 24 mini sausages in total. Unroll the puff pastry and cut into two long strips, then cut those into 12 shorter strips.

Time to assemble. Dunk a chipolata in the honey and mustard sauce, making sure it is covered all over. Wrap a piece of pastry around it, then lay it on the baking tray. Repeat with all the chipolatas.

Brush the pigs in blankets with the egg, then bake in the oven for 20–30 minutes until sticky and golden.

Chia seed jam twists

MAKES 12

These chia seed jam twists are a great snack for kids. They're full of good stuff from the berries and chia seeds, and make a satisfying sweet treat.

225g (8oz) strawberries, quartered
2 teaspoons honey
3 tablespoons milled chia seeds
1 x 320g (11¼oz) sheet of puff pastry
1 egg, beaten
2 teaspoons demerara sugar

Preheat the oven to 180°C/160°C fan/350°F and line a baking tray with baking parchment.

Add the strawberries to a bowl and use a fork to mash them until no large chunks remain. Mix in the honey and chia seeds, then set aside to thicken for 10 minutes.

Unroll the pastry and spread the strawberry jam over one half, then fold the other half of the pastry on top of it as if you are closing a book. Transfer to the freezer for 15–20 minutes to firm up.

After this time, cut the pastry into 12 strips. Twist each strip a couple of times, then place on the baking tray. Brush the twists with the egg, sprinkle with the demerara sugar and bake in the oven for 20–30 minutes until golden and puffed up.

Chocolate and custard twists

MAKES 8

Make these and eat them warm from the oven and you'll feel very smug. Try adding some chopped nuts or raisins, if you like.

150g (5oz) shop-bought custard
1 tablespoon cornflour (cornstarch)
1 teaspoon vanilla bean paste
1 x 320g (11¼oz) sheet of puff pastry
50g (2oz) chocolate chips (your preferred chocolate)
1 egg, beaten
Icing (confectioner's) sugar, to dust

Preheat the oven to 180°C/160°C/350°F and line a baking tray with baking parchment.

Whisk the custard with the cornflour and vanilla bean paste until smooth.

Unroll the puff pastry and lay it out vertically, then spread the custard over the bottom half and sprinkle over the chocolate chips. Lift the top half and fold down over the bottom half, then transfer to the freezer for 15–20 minutes to firm up.

Remove from the freezer and cut into eight strips, then twist each one two times before laying on the baking tray. Brush with the beaten egg and transfer to the oven to cook for 20–25 minutes until golden.

Leave to cool slightly, then dust with icing sugar to serve.

Cinnamon twists

MAKES 8

This hits the spot when you want a cinnamon roll without the effort of making dough. The tahini cream cheese is so good, so be generous with it!

60g (2½oz) unsalted butter, softened
1 tablespoon ground cinnamon
60g (2½oz) soft light brown sugar
1 x 320g (11¼oz) sheet of puff pastry
1 egg, beaten
40g (1½oz) cream cheese
40g (1½oz) icing (confectioner's) sugar
15g (½oz) tahini
1 teaspoon vanilla extract

Preheat the oven to 200°C/180°C fan/400°F and line a baking tray with baking parchment.

Mix the butter, cinnamon and brown sugar together until well combined. Unroll the puff pastry and spread the cinnamon butter all over, then fold in half as if you're closing a book, and cut into eight strips. Working quickly so the pastry doesn't get too warm, lift a strip and twist it whilst wrapping it around your fingers. Tuck the end underneath the twist, then place on the lined baking tray. Repeat this with the remaining strips. Brush the cinnamon twists with the egg and bake in the oven for 25–30 minutes, or until golden.

While they cook, make the tahini cream cheese glaze. First, beat the cream cheese until softened, then whisk in the icing sugar until smooth. Add the tahini and vanilla and mix again, loosening with a splash of water to make it just thin enough to dunk.

Remove the cinnamon twists from the oven, leave to cool slightly, then dunk into the tahini cream cheese glaze to cover. Set aside to cool a little more before serving.

Pistachio and honey twists

MAKES 8

These sweet and sticky pastries are inspired by the flavours of baklava and are a speedy sweet treat.

150g (5oz) pistachios, finely chopped

40g (1½oz) honey, plus 2 tablespoons

20g (¾oz) soft light brown sugar

40g (1½oz) unsalted butter, softened

1 teaspoon ground cinnamon

2 tablespoons rose or orange blossom water

1 x 320g (11¼oz) sheet of puff pastry

1 egg, beaten

Preheat the oven to 180°C/160°C fan/350°F and line a baking tray with baking parchment.

Mix the pistachios, 40g (1½oz) honey, sugar, butter, cinnamon and rose or orange blossom water until well combined.

Unroll the puff pastry sheet and lay out vertically, then spread the pistachio mix over the bottom half. Lift the top half of the pastry and fold down to cover, pressing down gently to seal. Cut into eight strips, then twist each one two times and place onto the baking tray. Brush with the beaten egg then transfer to the oven and bake for 20–25 minutes until golden and puffed up.

Meanwhile, mix the 2 tablespoons of honey with a splash of boiling water to loosen.

Remove the pistachio twists from the oven and brush with the honey syrup to finish.

ROLL IT

Ultimate sausage roll

SERVES 10–12

This recipe is my dream sausage roll. With sausage meat and bacon, sweet onion chutney, sage and hot English mustard, it's decadent and full of flavour.

600g (1lb 5oz) sausages

8 rashers streaky bacon, chopped

15 fresh sage leaves, roughly chopped

4 tablespoons caramelised onion chutney

1 x 320g (11¼oz) sheet of puff pastry

1–2 tablespoons English mustard, depending on preference

1 egg, beaten

1 tablespoon fennel seeds

Salt and freshly ground black pepper, to taste

Preheat the oven to 200°C/180°C fan/400°F and line a baking tray with baking parchment.

Use a sharp knife to make a cut into the casing of the sausages, then peel and discard them. Add the sausage meat to a mixing bowl along with the bacon, sage, chutney and a generous amount of salt and pepper. Mix until very well combined.

Unroll the puff pastry sheet and lay out horizontally, then spread the mustard all over. Add the sausage mixture just south of the middle of the pastry, then lift the top edge over to seal. Use a fork to seal the edge, then score diagonal lines across the top. Alternatively, make a plait. Add the sausage mixture in a vertical line down the centre of the pastry sheet. Use a knife to cut the pastry either side of the mixture into 2cm (¾in) diagonal strips, then start plaiting, folding alternate strips over the mixture and tucking the ends in to seal.

Brush all over with the beaten egg, then sprinkle over the fennel seeds. Transfer to the oven and bake for 30–40 minutes until the pastry is a deep golden. Leave to cool slightly before cutting into 10–12 slices.

Pork and hoisin sausage rolls

MAKES 16

My old flatmate, Chloe, used to make sticky hoisin chipolatas for every potluck or special occasion when we were at university. I still think they're the best party snack, and this is my version of them in sausage roll form.

400g (14oz) sausages
3 spring onions (scallions), thinly sliced
Thumb-sized piece of ginger, finely grated
1 red chilli, finely chopped
4 tablespoons hoisin sauce
2 tablespoons wholegrain mustard
1 x 320g (11¼oz) sheet of puff pastry
1 egg, beaten
1 tablespoon sesame seeds, a mix of black and white is nice
Salt and freshly ground black

Preheat the oven to 200°C/180°C fan/400°F and line a baking tray with baking parchment.

Use a sharp knife to make a cut into the casing of the sausages, then peel and discard them. Add the sausage meat to a bowl with the spring onions, ginger and chilli, then mix well with your hands to combine. Add the hoisin sauce and mustard and mix again, then season with a little salt and pepper.

Unroll the puff pastry sheet and cut it in half lengthways so you have two long strips of pastry. Using your hands, spread half the pork mix along the middle of one of the pastry strips in a cylinder. Brush the edge of the pastry closest to you with the beaten egg before folding over and sealing over the top of the sausage meat to meet the other edge, pressing a fork along the full length to seal. Repeat this with the other half.

Cut each long sausage roll into eight mini ones, then transfer to the lined baking tray. Brush with the beaten egg and sprinkle with the sesame seeds, then bake in the oven for 30–35 minutes until golden.

Chicken, cheese and kimchi rolls

MAKES 16

Something different when you want to make sausage rolls but feel like switching things up from a classic pork version. I love the addition of cheese and kimchi, making these really flavourful.

300g (10½oz) chicken mince (ground chicken)
400g (14oz) kimchi, drained and finely chopped
75g (3oz) Cheddar, grated
75g (3oz) low-moisture mozzarella, grated
2 spring onions (scallions), thinly sliced
1 tablespoon soy sauce
1 tablespoon sesame oil
1 x 320g (11¼oz) sheet of puff pastry
1 egg, beaten
1 tablespoon sesame seeds
Salt, to taste

Preheat the oven to 200°C/180°C fan/400°F and line a baking tray with baking parchment.

Add the chicken mince, kimchi, cheeses, spring onions, soy sauce, sesame oil and a little salt to a large bowl and mix well with your hands until combined.

Unroll the puff pastry sheet and cut it in half lengthways so you have two long strips of pastry. Using your hands, spread half the chicken mix along the middle of one of the pastry strips in a cylinder. Brush the edge of the pastry closest to you with the beaten egg before folding over and sealing over the top of the meat to meet the other edge, pressing a fork along the full length to seal. Repeat this with the other half.

Cut each long sausage into eight mini ones, then gently lift onto a lined baking tray. Brush them with the beaten egg, then sprinkle over the sesame seeds. Transfer to the oven and bake for 30–35 minutes until golden.

Caesar-ish salad with puffed Parmesan croutons

SERVES 4

Mix things up the next time you make a Caesar salad and make puff pastry croutons instead of using bread. If you're a real anchovy lover you could throw those in there too.

1 x 320g (11¼oz) sheet of puff pastry

80g (3oz) Parmesan, finely grated, plus a little extra to serve

1 egg, beaten

100g (3½oz) thick Greek yoghurt

60g (2½oz) mayonnaise

1 garlic clove, minced

½ tablespoon Dijon mustard

Juice of ½ lemon

500g (17½oz) leftover chicken, cut into bite-sized pieces

3 heads of romaine, leaves separated and chopped

Salt and freshly ground black pepper, to taste

Preheat the oven to 180°C/160°C fan/350°F and line a baking tray with baking parchment.

Unroll the puff pastry and lay it out horizontally, still on its paper from the packet. Scatter 30g (1oz) of the grated Parmesan all over, then roll up into a log as tightly as you can. Cut this into 32 equal-sized pieces, then lay onto the lined baking tray. Brush each one with the beaten egg and bake in the oven for 10 minutes. Remove and sprinkle with 10g (¼oz) grated Parmesan, then return to the oven for a final 8–10 minutes until golden.

Meanwhile, make the Caesar dressing by mixing together the yoghurt, mayonnaise, garlic, mustard, and remaining Parmesan, along with a a good squeeze of lemon juice, a couple dozen grinds of pepper and a little salt. Taste, adding more lemon juice, salt or pepper if needed. Add the chicken and romaine to a bowl and toss with the dressing until well combined.

Allow the croutons to cool before adding them to the salad. Serve with an extra grating of Parmesan and plenty of black pepper.

Ham, cheese and pesto pinwheels

MAKES 8

1 x 320g (11¼oz) sheet of puff
  pastry
2 tablespoons pesto
14 slices of thin-cut ham
80g (3oz) Cheddar, grated
1 egg, beaten

These are a great snack or prepable lunch. Try using different types of pesto and cheese to mix it up!

Preheat the oven to 200°C/180°C fan/400°F and line a baking tray with baking parchment.

Unroll the pastry sheet vertically in front of you and spread the pesto all over. Lay the ham slices on top, overlapping slightly as needed, then sprinkle the cheese on top. Roll the pastry sheet up as tightly as you can into a log. Cut into eight swirls, then lay on the baking tray. Brush with the beaten egg and bake in the oven for 25–30 minutes until golden.

Lamb and feta rolls

MAKES 16

These spicy rolls are another great twist on a classic. Use halloumi instead of feta if you prefer!

300g (10½oz) lamb mince (ground lamb)
200g (7oz) feta, crumbled
½ small red onion, finely chopped
2 tablespoons harissa paste
1 tablespoon dried mint
1 teaspoon ground cumin
1 teaspoon ground coriander
1 x 320g (11¼oz) sheet of puff pastry
1 egg, beaten
1 tablespoon coriander seeds, crushed
Salt, to taste

Preheat the oven to 200°C/180°C fan/400°F and line a baking tray with baking parchment.

Add the lamb mince, feta, red onion, harissa, mint, cumin and coriander to a mixing bowl and combine well with your hands. Season with a generous pinch of salt.

Unroll the puff pastry sheet and cut it in half lengthways so you have two long strips of pastry. Using your hands, spread half the lamb mix along the middle of one of the pastry strips in a cylinder. Brush the edge closest to you with the beaten egg, then lift one of the pastry edges over the top of the meat to meet the other edge, pressing a fork along the full length to seal. Repeat this with the other half.

Cut each long sausage into eight mini ones, then gently lift onto the lined baking tray. Brush them with the beaten egg, then sprinkle over the coriander seeds. Transfer to the oven and bake for 30–35 minutes until golden.

Spinach and potato rolls

MAKES 16

A delicious plant-based sausage roll option. Flavour with whatever curry paste you have in the fridge.

200g (7oz) spinach

50g (2oz) frozen peas

350g (12oz) tinned or leftover boiled potatoes, drained

3 tablespoons curry paste of choice

50g (2oz) peanuts, roughly chopped

20g (¾oz) coriander (cilantro), roughly chopped

1 x 320g (11¼oz) sheet of puff pastry (check the packet for vegan)

2 tablespoons plant-based milk

Salt, to taste

Preheat the oven to 200°C/180°C fan/400°F and line a baking tray with baking parchment.

Add the spinach to a colander and place in the sink. Boil the kettle, then pour the water over the spinach to wilt the leaves. Run them under cold water to cool, then drain and squeeze out as much liquid from the leaves as you can and finely chop.

Add the potatoes to a mixing bowl and use a fork to crush them until there are no big lumps. Season generously with salt, then add the chopped spinach, curry paste, peanuts, coriander and peas and mix well to combine.

Unroll the puff pastry sheet and cut it in half lengthways so you have two long strips of pastry. Using your hands, spread half the potato mix along the middle of one of the pastry strips in a cylinder. Brush the edge closest to you with milk and lift one of the pastry edges over the top of the filling to meet the other edge, pressing a fork along the full length to seal. Repeat this with the other half.

Cut each long sausage into eight mini ones, then gently lift onto a lined baking tray. Brush them with the milk, then bake in the oven for 30–35 minutes until golden.

Everything bagel, cream cheese and dill swirls

MAKES 8

Inspired by a sensational south London bakery called TOAD, these swirls are full of flavour from the everything bagel seasoning. They're also a great vehicle for lots of dill, which I really love.

160g (5½oz) cream cheese
2 spring onions (scallions), thinly sliced
2 tablespoons everything bagel seasoning, plus 2 teaspoons
15g (½oz) fresh dill, picked
1 x 320g (11¼oz) sheet of puff pastry
1 egg, beaten

Preheat the oven to 200°C/180°C fan/400°F and line a baking tray with baking parchment.

Mix the cream cheese, spring onions, 2 tablespoons everything bagel seasoning and most of the dill together in a bowl. Unroll the puff pastry vertically in front of you and spread the cream cheese mixture all over. Roll up as tightly as you can into a log. Cut into eight swirls, then lay them on the baking tray.

Brush with the beaten egg, then sprinkle the 2 teaspoons everything seasoning over the top. Bake for 25–30 minutes, then top with the reserved dill to finish.

Cardamom sugar palmiers

MAKES 14

This recipe is one where the result is much greater than the sum of its parts. Just a sheet of puff pastry, sugar and a few cardamom pods, and you have these caramelised, crunchy biscuits that are delicious with a cup of tea or coffee.

50g (2oz) caster (superfine) sugar
15 cardamom pods, seeds removed and ground
1 x 320g (11¼oz) sheet of puff pastry

Preheat the oven to 200°C/180°C fan/400°F and line a baking tray with baking parchment.

Mix the sugar and ground cardamom together in a bowl. Unroll the puff pastry and lay out horizontally, still on its paper from the packet. Scatter most of the cardamom sugar over the top, then use a rolling pin to gently press the sugar into the pastry as best you can.

Use a sharp knife to make a small slit halfway up the short side of the pastry to indicate the middle. Starting with the side closest to you, gently roll the pastry as tightly as you can up to the middle point. Twist the paper so the unrolled side is now closest to you, then roll that up tightly to meet the other half. Transfer to the fridge for 15–20 minutes to firm up.

Cut into 14 even slices, then lay them on your baking tray. Use your hands to gently press down on the palmiers to flatten slightly, then sprinkle the reserved sugar over the top. Bake in the oven for 18–20 minutes, flipping halfway. Leave to cool before serving.

Tiramisu wheels

MAKES 8

I love the combination of the flaky, caramelised pastry and the cold, whipped mascarpone in this recipe. Dust liberally with cocoa powder and you've got something really special from little effort.

40g (1½oz) unsalted butter, softened
2 teaspoons instant espresso powder
60g (2½oz) soft light brown sugar
1 x 320g (11¼oz) sheet of puff pastry
1 egg, beaten
100g (3½oz) mascarpone
100ml (3½fl oz) double (heavy) cream
1½ tablespoons coffee liqueur (I like Kahlúa)
Cocoa powder, to dust

Preheat the oven to 200°C/180°C fan/400°F and line a baking tray with baking parchment.

Mix the butter, espresso powder and sugar together until well combined. Unroll the puff pastry sheet and lay it out vertically. Spread all over with the espresso butter, then roll it up as tightly as you can into a log. Cut into eight swirls and lay them on the baking tray. Brush with the beaten egg and bake in the oven for 20–25 minutes until golden. Remove and leave to cool completely.

Once the pastries have cooled, make the topping. Add the mascarpone, cream and coffee liqueur to a bowl and whip to soft peaks. Add a dollop of this onto each pastry, then dust generously with cocoa powder to serve.

IT

Cheesy buffalo bean melts

MAKES 4

I love beans, as anyone who knows me is well aware. These pastries are filled with classic baked beans that are made a little spicy with the addition of hot sauce. I love the blue cheese here, but you can switch it to Cheddar or mozzarella if you prefer.

240g (9oz) baked beans
1–2 tablespoons hot sauce
1 x 320g (11¼oz) sheet of puff
  pastry
80g (3oz) blue cheese
1 egg, beaten

Preheat the oven to 200°C/180°C fan/400°F and line a baking tray with baking parchment.

Mix the baked beans with the hot sauce. Unroll the puff pastry and cut it lengthways into two strips, making one 1cm (½in) bigger than the other. Cut each of those strips into four rectangles.

Divide the beans between the four slightly smaller rectangles, piling them into the middle to leave a border. Crumble the blue cheese on top, brush the border with the beaten egg, then gently lay the slightly larger rectangles on top. Use a fork to press down around the border and seal the pastries into four parcels, then cut three small incisions on the top of each. Brush with the beaten egg and bake in the oven for 20–25 minutes until golden and puffed up.

Chicken, ham and tarragon hand pies

MAKES 6

Make these the next time you have leftover roast chicken. I like to serve them for lunch with a hot bowl of soup.

180g (6oz) leftover chicken, shredded
60g (2½oz) ham, torn
50g (2oz) frozen peas
2 tablespoons Dijon mustard
150g (5oz) crème fraîche
4 sprigs of fresh tarragon, leaves picked and chopped
Juice of ½ lemon
1 x 320g (11¼oz) sheet of puff pastry
1 egg, beaten
Salt and freshly ground black pepper, to taste

Preheat the oven to 200°C/180°C fan/400°F and line a baking tray with baking parchment.

Mix the chicken, ham, peas, mustard, crème fraîche, tarragon and lemon juice together until well combined, seasoning generously with salt and pepper.

Unroll the puff pastry and roll it out slightly to make it bigger. Cut lengthways into two long strips, then cut each strip into three squares. Divide the chicken mixture between the squares, leaving a border. Brush around the filling with the egg, then fold the pastries into triangles. Use a fork to seal the edges, then transfer to the baking tray.

Use a knife to cut a small incision in the top of each pie, then brush with the beaten egg. Bake in the oven for 20–25 minutes until golden.

Sausage and broccoli pies

SERVES 4

Serve these mini pies with mashed potato and peas for a cosy winter meal.

150g (5oz) crème fraîche
50g (2oz) Parmesan, finely grated
Juice of ½ lemon
A good grating of nutmeg
80g (3oz) broccoli, finely chopped
1 red chilli, thinly sliced
1 x 320g (11¼oz) sheet of puff pastry
200g (7oz) sausages, skin discarded
2 tablespoons extra virgin olive oil
1 egg, beaten
Salt and freshly ground black pepper, to taste

Preheat the oven to 200°C/180°C fan/400°F and line a baking tray with baking parchment.

Mix the crème fraîche, Parmesan, lemon juice and nutmeg, then season to taste with salt and pepper. Add the broccoli and chilli and mix again to combine.

Unroll the puff pastry and cut it lengthways into two strips, making one 1cm (½in) bigger than the other. Cut each of those strips into four rectangles.

Divide the sausage meat between the four smaller pieces of pastry and press into the pastry with the back of a spoon to make an even layer, leaving a 1cm (½in) border around the edge of the sausage meat. Spoon the broccoli and crème fraîche mixture on top of the sausage meat. Brush the pastry border with the beaten egg, then lay the bigger rectangles on top. Use a fork to press down all around the edge to seal the pastries, then cut three small incisions on the top of each. Brush all over with the egg and bake in the oven for 20–25 minutes until golden and puffed up.

Chipotle tofu and corn hand pies

MAKES 6

These smoky and spicy hand pies are totally plant-based and full of flavour. Delicious served hot or cold, they are great for lunch or packed as a nourishing snack.

200g (7oz) extra-firm tofu, coarsely grated

100g (3½oz) tinned sweetcorn

1 tablespoon chipotle paste

1 tablespoon tomato ketchup

1 tablespoon extra virgin olive oil

1 teaspoon paprika

2 spring onions (scallions), thinly sliced

Small handful of fresh coriander (cilantro), finely chopped

1 x 320g (11¼oz) sheet of puff pastry (check the packet for vegan)

2 tablespoons plant-based milk

Salt and freshly ground black pepper, to taste

Preheat the oven to 200°C/180°C fan/400°F and line a baking tray with baking parchment.

Add the tofu, sweetcorn, chipotle paste, ketchup, olive oil, paprika, spring onions and coriander to a bowl along with some salt and pepper. Mix well to combine.

Unroll the puff pastry and roll it out slightly to make it a bit bigger. Cut lengthways into two long strips, then cut each strip into three squares. Divide the tofu mixture between the squares, leaving some space around the edge. Brush around the filling with the milk, then fold over the pastry to make triangular parcels. Use a fork to seal the edges, then transfer to the lined baking tray.

Use a knife to make a small incision on the top of each pie, then brush all over with the milk. Transfer to the oven and bake for 20–25 minutes until golden and puffed up.

Fish en croute

MAKES 2 (to serve 2 or 4, depending how hungry!)

A great weeknight dinner that feels fancy yet comes together really quickly. Use good-quality fish and serve with buttered peas on the side.

100g (3½oz) baby spinach
1 x 320g (11¼oz) sheet of puff pastry
100g (3½oz) garlic and herb cheese (I like Boursin)
2 chunky cod fillets, approx. 160g (5½oz) each
Juice of ½ lemon
Small handful of fresh basil, leaves picked
1 egg, beaten
Salt and freshly ground black pepper, to taste

Preheat the oven to 180°C/160°C fan/350°F and line a baking tray with baking parchment.

Add the spinach to a colander and place in the sink. Boil the kettle, then pour the water over the spinach to wilt the leaves. Run under cold water to cool, then drain and squeeze out as much liquid from it as you can.

Unroll the puff pastry and cut lengthways into two strips, making one 1cm (½in) bigger than the other. Cut each strip into half so you have four rectangles in total.

Spread the garlic and herb cheese over the centre of the two smaller puff pastry squares, leaving a 2cm (¾in) border right round the edge. Top with half the spinach on each, then lay the fish on top. Squeeze over the lemon juice, season with salt and pepper and add a few basil leaves on top of the fish, then place the slightly larger pieces of pastry on top and press the edges down with a fork to seal. Make three small incisions in the top of both parcels, then transfer to the baking tray.

Brush all over with the beaten egg and bake in the oven for 20–25 minutes until golden.

Crab and tomato vol-au-vents

MAKES 12

Vol-au-vents are nostalgic, chic and, ultimately, a vehicle for your favourite ingredients and flavours. Make these when tomatoes are at their best and serve as a canapé for something special.

1 x 320g (11¼oz) sheet of puff pastry
1 egg, beaten
200g (7oz) white crab meat
40g (1½oz) mayonnaise
40g (1½oz) thick Greek yoghurt
Juice of 1 lemon
2 tomatoes, the best quality you can get, cut into pieces
Small bunch of fresh chives, finely chopped
Salt and freshly ground black pepper, to taste

Preheat the oven to 200°C/180°C fan/400°F and line a baking tray with baking parchment.

Unroll the puff pastry and cut lengthwise into three long strips. Cut each strip into four squares, then use a knife to score a smaller square inside each square, leaving a ½cm (¼in) border right round the edge, being careful not to cut all the way through. Place on the baking tray then brush them all over with the beaten egg. Bake in the oven for 15 minutes until golden and puffed up.

In the meantime, make the crab filling. Mix the crab meat with the mayonnaise, Greek yoghurt, the juice of ½ lemon and some salt and pepper. Taste, adding more lemon juice, salt and pepper as needed.

Remove the vol-au-vents from the oven and leave to cool down. Use a knife to remove the middle bit of pastry from each one and discard.

Lay a slice of tomato inside each vol au vent, then top with the dressed crab. Garnish with chives to serve.

Cream cheese and olive straws

MAKES 12

Serve these as a snack with pre-dinner drinks. They also pack up well for a picnic or potluck!

1 x 320g (11¼oz) sheet of puff pastry
100g (3½oz) cream cheese
4 tablespoons olive tapenade
Zest of ½ lemon
3 sprigs of fresh thyme, leaves picked
1 egg, beaten
2 tablespoons coriander seeds, crushed

Preheat the oven to 200°C/180°C fan/400°F and line a baking tray with baking parchment.

Unroll the puff pastry and spread the cream cheese all over. Spread the tapenade over the top, then sprinkle over the lemon zest and scatter the thyme leaves all over. Fold the pastry in half like a book, then press down gently to seal. Slice into 12 strips and transfer to the baking tray.

Brush with the beaten egg and sprinkle over the coriander seeds. Bake for 20–25 minutes until golden and puffed up.

Jalapeño poppers

MAKES 20

These are incredibly moreish and might convert you from the deep-fried kind. Skip the chorizo, if you like.

10 jalapeños, halved and deseeded
200g (7oz) cream cheese
60g (2½oz) chorizo, very finely chopped
40g (1½oz) Cheddar, finely grated
1 x 320g (11¼oz) sheet of puff pastry
1 egg, beaten
Salt and freshly ground black pepper, to taste

Preheat the oven to 200°C/180°C fan/400°F and line a baking tray with baking parchment.

Mix the cream cheese, chorizo and Cheddar in a bowl until combined, then season with a little salt and black pepper. Add a teaspoon of this mix into each jalapeño half, smoothing the top so they aren't overfilled.

Unroll the pastry onto a clean surface and cut it into four long strips, then cut each strip into five squares. To assemble, turn a pastry square so you are looking at a diamond shape and lay a jalapeño half down the middle, cut-side down. Fold the pastry up from either side so the corners meet to encase the jalapeño. Repeat with the remaining squares.

Brush the pastry all over with the beaten egg, then transfer to the oven and bake for 20–25 minutes until the pastry is puffed up and golden. Serve while hot.

Courgette, spinach and feta herb pies

MAKES 6

These are great for using up leftover bits from the fridge. Switch the spinach for kale, substitute the herbs to suit what you have, and use a different cheese if you like, too. I actually prefer to eat these once they have cooled, so they make a great packed lunch or snack.

100g (3½oz) spinach
200g (7oz) courgette (zucchini), coarsely grated
1 spring onion (scallion), thinly sliced
1 garlic clove, minced
10g (¼oz) fresh dill, roughly chopped
10g (¼oz) fresh mint, roughly chopped
1 teaspoon Aleppo chilli flakes
2 eggs
80g (3oz) feta
1 x 320g (11¼oz) sheet of puff pastry
Salt and freshly ground black pepper, to taste

Preheat the oven to 200°C/180°C fan/400°F and line a baking tray with baking parchment.

Add the spinach to a colander and place in the sink. Boil the kettle, then pour the water over the spinach to wilt the leaves. Run under cold water to cool, then drain and squeeze out as much liquid from it as you can and finely chop. Next, place the grated courgette inside a cheesecloth or J-cloth and squeeze out as much liquid as you can.

Add the courgette and spinach to a bowl along with the spring onion, garlic, herbs, chilli flakes and one of the eggs, then crumble in the feta and mix well to combine, adding a little salt and pepper too. Beat the other egg in a small bowl.

Unroll the puff pastry and roll it out slightly to make it a bit bigger. Cut lengthways into two long strips, then cut each strip into three squares. Divide the courgette mixture between the squares, leaving a 1cm (½in) border around the edge. Brush around the filling with the beaten egg, then fold over the pastry to make triangular parcels. Use a fork to seal the edges, then transfer to the lined baking tray.

Cut a small incision on the top of each pie, then brush all over with the egg. Bake for 20–25 minutes until golden.

See images on pages 106–107.

Stem ginger, berry and mascarpone puffs

MAKES 6

These are perfect in the warmer months and feel quite fancy while requiring minimal effort. I love the combination of the stem ginger and zingy lime with sweet summer berries – they're fresh and indulgent all at once. If you don't have a piping bag, you can use a ziplock one instead and cut a small hole in the corner to pipe, or alternatively just use a spoon.

1 x 320g (11¼oz) sheet of puff pastry
1 egg, beaten
2 tablespoons demerara sugar
150g (6oz) blackberries, strawberries, raspberries or blueberries
Zest and juice of ½ lime
2 balls of stem ginger, finely chopped
150ml (5 fl oz) double (heavy) cream
150g (5oz) mascarpone
3 tablespoons stem ginger syrup (from the jar)

Preheat the oven to 200°C/180°C fan/400°F and line a baking tray with baking parchment.

Unroll the puff pastry and roll it out slightly to make it a bit bigger. Cut the pastry in half lengthways, then cut each strip into three. Fold each square in half to make a triangle, not worrying if the edges don't line up exactly. Transfer these onto the lined baking tray, then brush them all over with the beaten egg. Sprinkle the demerara sugar on top, and transfer to the oven for 20–25 minutes until golden and puffed up.

Meanwhile, add the berries to a bowl, cutting any larger ones in half. Add the zest and juice of the lime, followed by the chopped stem ginger and mix well to combine. Set aside.

In a large mixing bowl, whip the double cream, mascarpone and stem ginger syrup to soft peaks. You want it to be strong enough to pipe, but not too stiff. Transfer to a piping bag, using a nozzle if you would like.

Remove the pastries from the oven and leave them to cool completely. To finish, cut the puffs open, pipe the mascarpone cream in a zig-zag inside each puff, then top with the berry mixture and some of the berry juice. Eat straight away.

Coconut and passionfruit vol-au-vents

MAKES 12

These sweet vol-au-vents use simple ingredients and can be adapted to suit whatever fruit is in season.

1 x 320g (11¼oz) sheet of puff pastry
1 egg, beaten
200g (7oz) double (heavy) cream
400g (14oz) thick Greek yoghurt
2 tablespoons runny honey
1 tablespoon vanilla bean paste
6 passionfruit
30g (1oz) toasted coconut chips

Preheat the oven to 200°C/180°C fan/400°F and line a baking tray with baking parchment.

Unroll the puff pastry and cut lengthways into three long strips. Cut each strip into four squares, then use a knife to score a smaller square inside each square, leaving a ½cm (¼in) border right round the square, being careful not to cut all the way through. Place on the baking tray then brush them all over with the beaten egg. Transfer to the oven and bake for 15 minutes until golden and puffed up.

Meanwhile, mix the cream and yoghurt together until thick, then fold through the honey and vanilla bean paste. Cut the passionfruit in half and scoop out the pulp.

Remove the vol-au-vents from the oven and leave to cool completely. Use a knife to remove the middle piece of pastry from each one and discard.

Fill the vol-au-vents with the whipped yoghurt, then spoon over some passionfruit pulp. Finish with the toasted coconut and serve.

Berry turnovers

MAKES 6

These turnovers are so versatile. You can use whatever berries and citrus you have to hand and experiment with adding herbs and spices too, if you like. Frozen or fresh berries work equally well here, so you can enjoy these delicious turnovers all year round.

240g (9oz) berries of choice
20g (¾oz) caster (superfine) sugar
Zest of 1 lemon
1 x 320g (11¼oz) sheet of puff pastry
1 egg, beaten
2 tablespoons demerara sugar

Preheat the oven to 200°C/180°C fan/400°F and line a baking tray with baking parchment.

Mix the berries, sugar and lemon zest together in a bowl, mashing slightly with a fork.

Unroll the puff pastry and roll it out slightly to make it a bit bigger. Cut the pastry in half lengthways, then cut each strip into three. Divide the berry mixture between the six squares of pastry, spooning into the middle. Brush the pastry around the berries with the beaten egg, then lift one corner and fold over to make a triangle, pressing down along the edges gently to seal. Lift gently onto the baking tray, then repeat to make six pies in total.

Make a small incision on the top of each pastry, then brush all over with the egg. Sprinkle the demerara over the top, then transfer to the oven and bake for 20–25 minutes until golden. Allow to cool slightly before serving.

DECORATE

IT

Sage and anchovy bites

MAKES 8

These little pastries are great as a canapé – they're full of flavour and a fun thing to serve at a party. Thanks so much to my friend (and recipe taster!) Andrew for the idea when I was writing this book. These are quite punchy, so if you'd prefer a less intense anchovy taste, use half an anchovy per pastry instead.

1 x 320g (11¼oz) sheet of puff pastry
8 fresh sage leaves
80g (3oz) ricotta
8 anchovies
Zest of 1 lemon
1 egg, beaten

Preheat the oven to 200°C/180°C fan/400°F and line a baking tray with baking parchment.

Unroll the puff pastry sheet. Using an approximately 7cm (2¾in) long fish-shaped cookie cutter (or a knife and some artistic skill!), cut 16 fish from the pastry.

To assemble, lay a sage leaf on top of a piece of pastry, an anchovy on top of that and then top with a blob of ricotta. Finish with some lemon zest, then brush the border around the filling with the beaten egg. Lay another fish-shaped piece of pastry on top, then use a fork to seal the edges. Place on the baking tray and repeat with the remaining fish.

Brush the anchovy bites with the beaten egg, then bake in the oven for 10–15 minutes until golden brown and puffed up.

Prawn triangles

MAKES 24

Prawn toast-inspired flavours but with crispy pastry instead of bread. Not traditional, but still very delicious.

330g (11oz) raw king prawns (shrimps)
Thumb-sized piece of root ginger, grated
2 garlic cloves, minced
2 tablespoons sesame oil
2 tablespoons soy sauce
Zest and juice of 1 lime
1 egg white
4 spring onions (scallions), thinly sliced
1 x 320g (11¼oz) sheet of puff pastry
4 tablespoons sesame seeds (a mix of black and white is nice)

Preheat the oven to 200°C/180°C fan/400°F and line a baking tray with baking parchment.

Add half the prawns, the ginger, garlic, sesame oil, soy sauce, lime zest and egg white to a food processor and blitz until combined. Chop the remaining prawns then add those to the mix, along with the spring onions.

Unroll the puff pastry onto a clean surface. Use a sharp knife to cut the sheet vertically into four sections. Next, cut each strip into three squares, then each square into two triangles. Transfer half the triangles to a lined baking tray – you'll need to do this in two batches, so put the other half into the fridge to stay cold for now.

Spread the prawn mixture over the triangles, spreading it to the edge as much as you can. Sprinkle over the sesame seeds, then bake in the oven for 12–15 minutes. Squeeze the lime juice over to serve and eat them while they're hot, getting the next batch in the oven ready for seconds!

Upside-down leek tartlets

MAKES 4

Easy, delicious and quick: these tarts are a brilliant option for a weeknight dinner. Serve with salad in the warmer months, or green vegetables and mash when you want something more hearty and warming.

4 baby leeks, trimmed
100g (3½oz) cream cheese
2 tablespoons wholegrain mustard
3 tablespoons extra virgin olive oil
3 tablespoons sherry vinegar
1 x 320g (11¼oz) sheet of puff pastry
1 egg, beaten
40g (1½oz) pecorino, finely grated
20g (¾oz) pine nuts, toasted
Salt and freshly ground black pepper, to taste

Preheat the oven to 190°C/170°C fan/375°F and line a baking tray with baking parchment.

Halve each baby leek lengthways, then halve again to make four short pieces. Mix the cream cheese with the mustard and some salt and pepper.

Unroll the puff pastry onto a clean surface, then spread the cream cheese mixture over the pastry sheet. Cut into four equal-sized rectangles.

Combine the olive oil and vinegar in a small bowl with some salt, then dunk the leeks in to coat. Lay these out four in a row, cut-side down, on the baking tray, leaving enough space between them for a piece of pastry to be placed on top of each group. Lay a puff pastry square on top of each set of leeks, pressing the edges down with a fork. Brush all over with the egg, then bake in the oven for 20–30 minutes until the pastry is golden.

Remove from the oven and use a fish slice to get underneath the pastries and flip them over so the leeks are on top. Sprinkle over the pecorino and scatter with the pine nuts to serve.

Camembert wreath

SERVES 6–8

This recipe is really a suggestion for another way to eat baked Camembert. This is great for using old jars and spices from your kitchen – pick whatever flavours you like and feel free to dress up your cheese too.

1 x 250g (9oz) Camembert, packaging removed and box reserved

1 tablespoon extra virgin olive oil

1 x 320g (11¼oz) sheet of puff pastry

2 tablespoons sundried tomato paste, olive tapenade, pesto or harissa

1 egg, beaten

1 teaspoon za'atar

Preheat the oven to 200°C/180°C fan/400°F and line a baking tray with baking parchment.

Place the Camembert in the bottom part of its box and put it in the middle of the baking tray. Use a sharp knife to score a few incisions in the top of the cheese, then drizzle with a little olive oil.

Unroll the puff pastry and spread all over with the spread of your choice. Fold in half vertically, then cut into four strips. Working quickly, twist each strip of pastry and lay them onto the baking tray around the cheese, making a swirl by joining the end of one pastry twist with the start of the next. Brush all over with the egg and sprinkle over the za'atar. Bake in the oven for 20–25 minutes, or until the pastry is golden and the cheese is bubbling. Allow to cool slightly before transferring to a platter to serve.

Pop tarts

MAKES 4

These are a fun recipe for people of all ages. Get creative with different sprinkles, and experiment with different fillings; salted caramel, jam, nut spreads or butters are all delicious options.

100g (3½oz) raspberries
1 x 320g (11¼oz) sheet of puff pastry
4 tablespoons peanut butter
1 egg, beaten
50g (2oz) icing (confectioner's) sugar
Sprinkles, to decorate

Preheat the oven to 200°C/180°C fan/400°F and line a baking tray with baking parchment.

Mash the raspberries slightly in a bowl. Unroll the puff pastry and cut lengthways into two strips, making one 1cm (½in) bigger than the other. Cut each strip into four equal-sized pieces.

Divide the raspberries between the slightly smaller pastry pieces, spooning them into the middle and leaving a 1.5cm (¾in) border right round the square. Drizzle 1 tablespoon of peanut butter over the top of each pile of raspberries, then brush the border with the egg. Lay the slightly bigger pieces of pastry on top, pressing down around the edge with a fork to seal. Place onto the baking tray, brush all over with the egg and transfer to the oven to bake for 20–25 minutes.

In the meantime, make the icing. Mix the icing sugar with enough water to make a thick but drizzle-able consistency.

Remove the pop tarts from the oven and leave to cool completely. Drizzle over the icing and decorate with sprinkles to finish.

Lemon meringue tart

SERVES 6–8

This recipe couldn't be simpler, but it makes an impressive pudding that will satisfy any sweet tooth.

1 x 320g (11¼oz) sheet of puff pastry
1 egg, beaten
3 egg whites
½ teaspoon cream of tartar
100g (3½oz) caster (superfine) sugar
250g (9oz) lemon curd

Preheat the oven to 200°C/180°C fan/400°F and line a baking tray with baking parchment.

Unroll the puff pastry and use a small knife to score a roughly 2cm (¾in) border right round the sheet, being careful not to cut all the way through. Brush all over with the beaten egg, then transfer to the oven to bake for 20 minutes, or until puffed up and golden brown.

In the meantime, make the meringue. Add the egg whites and cream of tartar to the clean bowl of a stand mixer and whisk to soft peaks (you can also do this with an electric whisk). Once at this stage, start to add the sugar 1 tablespoon at a time while continuing to whisk, gradually increasing the speed as you add more sugar. Whisk until you have stiff peaks and your meringue mixture is nice and glossy.

Set the grill to medium-high. Use a spoon to push down the middle of the puff pastry where it has puffed up, then spread the lemon curd all over the middle. Pile on the meringue, using the back of a spoon to make nice peaks on top of the tart. Place under the grill for 2–3 minutes to toast the meringue – keep an eye on it so it doesn't burn!

Cut into slices to serve.

Plum and pistachio frangipane tart

SERVES 8–10

My grandma's favourite dessert is a pear and frangipane tart. Diverging from the classic a little here, I love the colour from the pistachios and using plums when they're in season.

1 x 320g (11¼oz) sheet of
puff pastry
75g (3oz) butter, softened
75g (3oz) caster (superfine)
sugar
2 eggs
75g (3oz) pistachios, blitzed
until ground
1 tablespoon plain
(all-purpose) flour
1–2 teaspoon almond extract
(optional)
8 plums, halved, stoned and
thinly sliced

Preheat the oven to 180°C/160°C fan/350°F and line a baking tray with baking parchment.

Unroll the puff pastry onto the lined baking tray and use a sharp knife to score a 2cm (¾in) border right round the sheet, being careful not to cut all the way through. Beat one of the eggs in a bowl and brush all over the pastry, then transfer to the oven for 10 minutes.

Meanwhile, prepare the frangipane. Beat the butter and sugar together for 2 minutes until light and fluffy, then add the remaining egg and mix again until well combined. Add the ground pistachios and flour and mix well. Finally, add the almond extract, if using, and mix one last time.

Remove the pastry from the oven and use a spoon to press the centre down where it has puffed up. Gently spread the frangipane over the middle, not worrying too much about breaking the pastry, but smoothing out as much as you can. Arrange the sliced plums as you like on top, fanning them as you go. Return to the oven for 20–25 minutes until the pastry is golden and the frangipane has risen.

Leave to cool before cutting into slices and serving with cream, custard or crème fraîche.

Chocolate and hazelnut flowers

MAKES 9

Chocolate hazelnut spread will always feel like such a treat to me. Encased here in the puff pastry and scattered with roasted hazelnuts, these little pastries are nostalgic and slightly more sophisticated than eating the spread straight from the jar.

1 x 320g (11¼oz) sheet of puff pastry
135g (4½oz) hazelnut chocolate spread (or a different chocolate/nut spread!)
1 egg, beaten
30g (1oz) blanched hazelnuts, chopped
Icing (confectioner's) sugar, to dust (optional)

Preheat the oven to 200°C/180°C fan/400°F and line a baking tray with baking parchment.

Unroll the puff pastry and cut it into nine equal-sized squares. Dollop the hazelnut chocolate spread into the middle of each one, then lift the edges of the square up and pinch together so the filling is completely sealed within the pastry. Flip over and use the palm of your hand to flatten the parcels, then use a small knife to cut five little incisions towards the centre to make petals. Transfer to the baking tray, then twist the petals so they are cut-side facing up.

Brush the flowers with the beaten egg, then sprinkle some chopped hazelnuts into the middle. Transfer to the oven and bake for 15–20 minutes until golden.

Remove from the oven and leave to cool before dusting with icing sugar to serve, if you like.

Almond croissant Christmas tree

SERVES 10–12

90g (3¼oz) unsalted butter,
   softened
90g (3¼oz) caster (superfine)
   sugar
2 eggs
90g (3¼oz) ground almonds
1 tablespoon plain
   (all-purpose) flour
1–2 teaspoons almond
   extract
2 x 320g (11¼oz) sheets of
   puff pastry
30g (1oz) flaked almonds
Icing (confectioner's) sugar,
   to serve

Make this on Christmas morning for a really special breakfast. It tastes like you've made fresh almond croissants but it takes a fraction of the time.

Preheat the oven to 200°C/180°C fan/400°F and line a baking tray with baking parchment.

First, make the frangipane. Beat the butter and sugar together for a couple of minutes until light and fluffy, then add 1 of the eggs and beat again until well incorporated. Add the ground almonds, flour and almond extract and mix again until smooth. Beat the other egg in a small bowl.

Unroll one of the puff pastry sheets onto the lined baking tray. Spread the majority of the frangipane over the whole sheet, reserving a couple of tablespoons, then top with the other pastry sheet and gently press them together around the edge to seal. Cut the pastry sheets into a Christmas tree shape – one long triangle with a chunky base at the bottom. Use a cookie cutter or knife to cut a star or other decoration from the cutaway pastry. Bake these offcuts for snacking… twist or roll it as you like!

To finish making the tree, score two lines down the length of the tree to indicate where the tree trunk is, being careful not to cut the whole way through. Then, start to cut branches either side of the trunk, about 2.5cm (1in) thick. Once all of the branches are cut, twist them a couple of times. Add the decoration to the top of the tree, then brush the whole thing with the reserved beaten egg. Spread the reserved frangipane down the trunk, then top with the flaked almonds. Bake in the oven to bake for 20–25 minutes, or until the pastry is golden brown and the frangipane on top has risen.

Remove from the oven and leave to cool slightly, then dust with icing sugar to serve.

Mince pie slices

MAKES 6

These are a speedy option that will satisfy any craving for a homemade mince pie, without making pastry or mincemeat. Serve warm with your favourite accompaniment – I like crème fraîche best.

1 x 320g (11¼oz) sheet of puff pastry, plus extra for decorating
420g (15oz) mincemeat (the sweet kind!)
1 egg, beaten
Icing (confectioner's) sugar, to dust (optional)

Preheat the oven to 200°C/180°C fan/400°F and line a baking tray with baking parchment.

Unroll the puff pastry sheet and cut into six equal-sized pieces. Score a 1cm (½in) border around the edge of each, then brush all over with the beaten egg. Transfer to the oven to prebake for an initial 10 minutes. If making any pastry decorations, cut these from another sheet of puff pastry now.

Remove from the oven and use the back of a spoon to press down the pastry where it has puffed up. Spoon the mincemeat over the centre, and top with your pastry decoration, if using. Brush the uncooked pastry with egg and return to the oven for a final 20–30 minutes until golden.

Dust with icing sugar to finish, if you like.

Index

A

almond croissant Christmas
tree 132
anchovies: anchovy, onion
and tomato tart 26
broccoli and anchovy
twists 59
sage and anchovy bites 116
apple crumble tart 44
asparagus: prosciutto and
asparagus twists with
dippy eggs 54

B

bacon: tartiflette 30
mushroom and egg tart 14
ultimate sausage roll 72
baked beans: cheesy buffalo
bean melts 92
banoffee tarts 39
beef: lahmacun-inspired
tart 38
berry, stem ginger and
mascarpone puffs 109
berry turnovers 113
broccoli: broccoli and
anchovy twists 59
sausage and broccoli
pies 95

C

Caesar salad with puffed
Parmesan croutons 77
Camembert wreath 122

caramel sauce: banoffee
tarts 39
cardamom sugar palmiers 87
carrots: spiced carrot and
whipped tofu tart 34
cheese: Camembert
wreath 122
cheese and chutney
twists 55
cheese and tomato
tartlets 21
cheesy buffalo bean
melts 92
chicken, cheese and
kimchi rolls 76
courgette and goat's
cheese tart 22
courgette, spinach and
feta herb pies 108
green chilli cheese swirl 48
halloumi and mango
chutney parcels 60
ham, cheese and pesto
pinwheels 79
lamb and feta rolls 81
mustard and Cheddar
twists 50
'nduja and Parmesan
twists 56
puffed Parmesan
croutons 77
pumpkin, blue cheese and
hazelnut tart 31

strawberry and goat's
cheese tart 42
tartiflette 30
triple cheese and
spinach pie 17
chia seed jam twists 63
chicken: Caesar salad 77
chicken, cheese and
kimchi rolls 76
chicken, ham and tarragon
hand pies 94
chillies: chipotle tofu and
corn hand pies 97
green chilli cheese swirl 48
jalapeño poppers 104
chocolate: chocolate and
custard twists 64
chocolate and hazelnut
flowers 130
Christmas tree, almond
croissant 132
chutney: cheese and
chutney twists 55
coriander chutney 34
cinnamon twists 67
coconut and passionfruit vol-
au-vents 110
coffee: tiramisu wheels 88
courgettes (zucchini):
courgette and goat's
cheese tart 22
courgette, spinach and
feta herb pies 108

crab and tomato vol-au-vents 101
cream: banoffee tarts 39
  peach galette with honey and yoghurt cream 41
  tiramisu wheels 88
cream cheese: cinnamon twists 67
  cream cheese and olive straws 103
  everything bagel, cream cheese and dill swirls 84
  hot smoked trout and cream cheese tart 18
  jalapeño poppers 104
  upside-down leek tartlets 120
croissant Christmas tree, almond 132
croutons, puffed Parmesan 77
custard: chocolate and custard twists 64

D
dill: everything bagel, cream cheese and dill swirls 84

E
eggs: mushroom and egg tart 14
  prosciutto and asparagus twists with dippy eggs 54
everything bagel, cream cheese and dill swirls 84

F
fish: anchovy, onion and tomato tart 26
  broccoli and anchovy twists 59
  fish en croute 98
  hot smoked trout and cream cheese tart 18
  roasted tomato and tuna tart 37
  sage and anchovy bites 116
flowers, chocolate and hazelnut 130
frangipane: plum and pistachio frangipane tart 129

G
galette, peach 41

H
halloumi and mango chutney parcels 60

ham: chicken, ham and tarragon hand pies 94
  ham, cheese and pesto pinwheels 79
hazelnuts: chocolate and hazelnut flowers 130
  pumpkin, blue cheese and hazelnut tart 31
herbs: courgette, spinach and feta herb pies 108
hoisin sauce: pork and hoisin sausage rolls 74
honey: honey mustard pigs in blankets 62
  peach galette with honey and yoghurt cream 41
  pistachio and honey twists 68

J
jalapeño poppers 104
jam: chia seed jam twists 63

K
kimchi: chicken, cheese and kimchi rolls 76

L
lahmacun-inspired tart 38
lamb and feta rolls 81
leeks: upside-down leek tartlets 120
lemon meringue tart 126
lettuce: Caesar salad 77

M

mango chutney: halloumi and mango chutney parcels 60

mascarpone: stem ginger, berry and mascarpone puffs 109

tiramisu wheels 88

meringue: lemon meringue tart 126

mince pie slices 135

mushroom and egg tart 14

mustard: honey mustard pigs in blankets 62

mustard and Cheddar twists 50

N

'nduja and Parmesan twists 56

O

olives: cream cheese and olive straws 103

onions: anchovy, onion and tomato tart 26

P

palmiers, cardamom sugar 87

passionfruit: coconut and passionfruit vol-au-vents 110

pastries: cheesy buffalo bean melts 92

halloumi and mango chutney parcels 60

pop tarts 125

sage and anchovy bites 116

peach galette with honey and yoghurt cream 41

pepperoni pizza tart 25

pesto: ham, cheese and pesto pinwheels 79

pies: chicken, ham and tarragon hand pies 94

chipotle tofu and corn hand pies 97

courgette, spinach and feta herb pies 108

fish en croute 98

sausage and broccoli pies 95

triple cheese and spinach pie 17

pinwheels: ham, cheese and pesto pinwheels 79

tiramisu wheels 88

pistachios: pistachio and honey twists 68

plum and pistachio frangipane tart 129

pizza tart, pepperoni 25

plum and pistachio frangipane tart 129

pop tarts 125

poppers, jalapeño 104

potatoes: green chilli cheese swirl 48

spinach and potato rolls 82

tartiflette 30

prawns (shrimp): prawn

triangles 119

prosciutto and asparagus twists 54

pumpkin, blue cheese and hazelnut tart 31

R

raspberries: pop tarts 125

ricotta: courgette and goat's cheese tart 22

rolls: chicken, cheese and kimchi rolls 76

lamb and feta rolls 81

pork and hoisin sausage rolls 74

spinach and potato rolls 82

ultimate sausage roll 72

S

sage and anchovy bites 116

salad, Caesar 77

sausages: honey mustard pigs in blankets 62

pork and hoisin sausage rolls 74

sausage and broccoli pies 95

ultimate sausage roll 72

smoked trout: hot smoked trout and cream cheese tart 18

spiced carrot and whipped tofu tart 34

spinach: courgette, spinach and feta herb pies 108

spinach and potato rolls 82

triple cheese and
spinach pie 17
strawberries: chia seed jam
twists 63
strawberry and goat's
cheese tart 42
straws, cream cheese and
olive 103
stem ginger, berry and
mascarpone puffs 109
sweetcorn: chipotle tofu and
corn hand pies 97
swirls: everything bagel,
cream cheese and dill
swirls 84
green chilli cheese swirl 48

T

tarragon: chicken, ham and
tarragon hand pies 94
tartlets: cheese and tomato
tartlets 21
upside-down leek
tartlets 120
tarts: anchovy, onion and
tomato tart 26
apple crumble tart 44
banoffee tarts 39
courgette and goat's
cheese tart 22
lahmacun-inspired tart 38
lemon meringue tart 126
mince pie slices 135
mushroom and egg tart 14
pepperoni pizza tart 25
plum and pistachio

frangipane tart 129
pumpkin, blue cheese and
hazelnut tart 31
roasted tomato and tuna
tart 37
spiced carrot and whipped
tofu tart with coriander
chutney 34
strawberry and goat's
cheese tart 42
tartiflette 30
tiramisu wheels 88
tofu: chipotle tofu and corn
hand pies 97
spiced carrot and whipped
tofu tart 34
tomatoes: anchovy, onion
and tomato tart 26
cheese and tomato
tartlets 21
crab and tomato
vol-au-vents 101
pepperoni pizza tart 25
roasted tomato and
tuna tart 37
trout: hot smoked trout and
cream cheese tart 18
tuna: roasted tomato and
tuna tart 37
turnovers, berry 113
twists: broccoli and anchovy
twists 59
cheese and chutney
twists 55
chia seed jam twists 63
chocolate and custard

twists 64
cinnamon twists 67
mustard and Cheddar
twists 50
'nduja and Parmesan
twists 56
pistachio and honey
twists 68
prosciutto and asparagus
twists 54

U

upside-down leek
tartlets 120

V

vol-au-vents: coconut and
passionfruit
vol-au-vents 110
crab and tomato
vol-au-vents 101

W

wreath, Camembert 122

Y

yoghurt: coconut and
passionfruit
vol-au-vents 110
peach galette with honey
and yoghurt cream 41

Acknowledgments

A huge thank you to my editor Issy for all of your support and patience over the course of this project. I couldn't believe it when you first emailed me with the idea for the book, and it still feels surreal! You have made this so fun and I am so, so grateful to you.

To the dreamy group of people who worked on the shoot - where do I begin?! Luke Albert, your calm energy and exquisite taste in music were so appreciated on our long shoot days. You made these recipes look so vibrant and beautiful. Louie Waller, your talent for props and eye for colours and patterns is magical and we all treasured every moment we got to have you on set! Claire Rochford, you have been so brilliant in designing the book. Thank you for trying so many options and making every page look so good. To Emma Cantlay, Georgia Rudd and Sadie Albuquerque - you were the most amazing assistants and I'm totally in awe of your skills. Thank you for keeping me calm and always being one step ahead of me. I feel so lucky to call you all friends as well as colleagues.

There are a whole load of people I have been lucky to work with and learn from over the past few years. Esther Clark, you took a chance on me and let me assist you and I am so glad that has turned into all these years of friendship and working together. You have taught me so much and continue to; I hope we will always get to cook and eat together. Saskia Sidey, thank you for guiding me through writing my first book and always championing us assistants! Nicola Lamb, thank you for being so generous with your expertise and encouragement – your teaching has been so instrumental to me getting to do this work and I'm so grateful. Olivia Cavalli, thank you for letting me test your recipes many years ago, I'm delighted to now call you a friend and am so appreciative of your support throughout writing this. Thank you to all of the other wonderful people I have had the pleasure of working with and learning from - you know who you are.

To my incredible friends - thank you for putting up with my chat about puff pastry for months, and for being excited for me when I was mostly just scared. You are the best people and I'm so grateful for you. Extra special thanks to those of you who tested and tasted recipes: Sas and Hec, Iz, Anya, Riccardo and Alice, Andrew and India, Sophie, Flo, Jenni and Sean, Lucy, Nicole and Emma - I couldn't have done it without you. Scarlett, thank you for being my live-in taste tester for many years and, most importantly, for being such a brilliant friend. Eating dinner together is the best.

A huge thank you to my parents. You have been nothing but supportive as I spent many years at university only to make an unexpected career change at the end of it. Thank you for testing my recipes, even though the exact temperature of your oven remains a guess! Grandma and Grandad - your support over the past few years has meant so much. Aunty Val, thank you for being a big piece of home here in London and for all your encouragement. Joe and Bronte - you rock, and the whole rest of our clan do too.

Grandma - you are the best friend and I will never tire of blethering away to you on the phone or over a game of scrabble. Thank you for bringing us into the kitchen; making Victoria sponges with you on the trolley are such happy memories. I love you and our shared love of food so much.

Author bio

Caitlin is a Scottish food stylist and recipe developer based in London. Having been obsessed with food for as long as she can remember, it wasn't until doing a pastry course during the 2020 lockdown that Caitlin decided to pursue a career in food. Whilst finishing her Masters in Gender Studies, she began assisting food stylists and recipe testing, and now works full time on cookbooks and other editorial and commercial food projects. Caitlin grew up baking with her Grandma, who she continues to consult regularly about recipes and what to cook for dinner.